Easy Diabetes Recipes for Busy People

How to Burn Fat with the Diabetes Cookbook

Evelin Turk

Table of Contents

Fruit-filled Meringues with Custard Sauce

Servings: 6

Ingredients:

2 large ripe kiwis, peeled and chopped

1 cup quartered fresh strawberries

1 cup fresh blueberries

Directions:

1. Prepare Meringue Cookies according to the instructions, but place the beaten egg white mixture on the prepared pan and use the back of a spoon to spread it into six 4-inch circles, creating indentations in the center of each one. Proceed with the recipe as directed.

2. Combine the kiwi, strawberries, and blueberries in a medium bowl and toss to mix well.

3. To assemble, place a baked meringue on each of 6 plates. Top each meringue with about 1/2 cup of the fruit mixture. Drizzle evenly with the sauce and serve at once.

Nutrition Info:

39 g carb, 194 cal, 2 g fat, 1 g sat fat, 71 mg chol, 2 g fib, 5 g pro, 79 mg sod • Carb Choices: 21/2; Exchanges: 2 carb, 1/2 fruit

Sauteed Chicken with Texas Spice Rub

Servings: 4

Ingredients:

1/2 teaspoon kosher salt

1/2 teaspoon chili powder

1/4 teaspoon ground cumin

1/8 teaspoon freshly ground pepper

4 (4-ounce) boneless skinless chicken breasts

2 teaspoons extra virgin olive oil

Lime wedges

Directions:

1. Stir together the salt, chili powder, cumin, and pepper in a small bowl. Sprinkle the chicken with the spice mixture.

2. Heat a large skillet over medium heat. Add the oil and tilt the pan to coat the bottom evenly. Add the chicken and cook, turning once, until the juices run clear, about 4 minutes on each side. Divide the chicken among 4 plates and serve at once with the lime wedges.

Nutrition Info:

0 g carb, 145 cal, 5 g fat, 1 g sat fat, 63 mg chol, 0 g fib, 23 g pro, 202 mg sod • Carb Choices: 0; Exchanges: 3 lean protein, 1/2 fat

Frozen Yogurt

Servings: 8

Ingredients:

1 cup 1% low-fat milk

3⁄4 cup sugar

2 cups plain low-fat yogurt

1⁄2 teaspoon vanilla extract

Directions:

1. Stir together the milk and sugar in a small saucepan. Cook over medium heat, stirring often, until the sugar dissolves, about 3 minutes (do not boil). Transfer to a small bowl and let cool to room temperature. Refrigerate, covered, until chilled, about 2 hours.

2. Whisk together the milk mixture, yogurt, and vanilla in a medium bowl until smooth. Spoon the mixture into an ice cream maker and freeze according to manufacturer's instructions. Transfer to an airtight container and freeze overnight. The yogurt can be frozen, covered, for up to 1 week.

Nutrition Info:

25 g carb, 125 cal, 1 g fat, 1 g sat fat, 5 mg chol, 0 g fib, 4 g pro, 56 mg sod • Carb Choices: 1 1/2; Exchanges: 1 1/2 carb

Panna Cotta

Servings: 6

Ingredients:

2 teaspoons canola oil

3 cups 2% low-fat milk, divided

1 tablespoon unflavored gelatin

1/2 cup sugar

1 tablespoon vanilla extract

Directions:

1. Brush six 6-ounce ramekins or custard cups with the oil.

2. Place 1 1/2 cups of the milk in a medium saucepan. Sprinkle with the gelatin and let stand 2 minutes to soften. Add the sugar and cook over medium heat, stirring constantly, until the mixture thickens and coats the back of a spoon (do not boil). Remove from the heat and stir in the remaining 1 1/2 cups milk and the vanilla. Divide the mixture among the prepared ramekins. Refrigerate the custards, covered, overnight.

3. To serve, loosen the edge of each panna cotta with a knife and invert the ramekins onto individual plates.

Nutrition Info:

23 g carb, 149 cal, 4 g fat, 2 g sat fat, 10 mg chol, 0 g fib, 5 g pro, 53 mg sod • Carb Choices: 1 1/2; Exchanges: 1 1/2 carb

Beef And Barley Chili

Servings: 6

Ingredients:

12 ounces 95% lean ground beef, crumbled

1 medium onion, chopped

1 medium green bell pepper, chopped

1 jalapeño, seeded and minced

3 garlic cloves, minced

2 1/2 tablespoons chili powder

1 tablespoon ground cumin

2 cups water

1 3/4 cups Beef Stock or low-sodium beef broth

1 (15-ounce) can no-salt-added red kidney beans, rinsed and drained

1 (14 1/2-ounce) can no-salt-added diced tomatoes

1/2 cup pearl barley

3 tablespoons no-salt-added tomato paste

1 tablespoon lime juice

Chopped fresh cilantro

Directions:

1. Combine the beef, onion, bell pepper, and jalapeño in a large saucepan. Place over medium heat and cook, stirring often, until the beef is browned, 5 minutes. Add the garlic, chili powder, and cumin and cook, stirring constantly, until fragrant, 30 seconds.

2. Add the water, stock, beans, tomatoes, barley, and tomato paste and bring to a boil. Reduce the heat to low, cover, and simmer until the barley is tender, yet firm to the bite, about 30 minutes. Remove from the heat and stir in the lime juice. Ladle the chili evenly into 6 bowls, sprinkle evenly with the cilantro, and serve at once. The chili can be frozen for up to 3 months.

Nutrition Info:

33 g carb, 262 cal, 6 g fat, 2 g sat fat, 37 mg chol, 10 g fib, 19 g pro, 228 mg sod •
Carb Choices: 2; Exchanges: 1 1/2 starch, 1 veg, 1 1/2 lean protein, 1/2 plant-based protein

Tapioca Pudding

Servings: 4

Ingredients:

2 cups 1% low-fat milk

1 large egg 1/3 cup sugar

3 tablespoons minute tapioca

1/8 teaspoon salt

1 teaspoon vanilla extract

Directions:

1. Combine the milk, egg, sugar, tapioca, and salt in a medium saucepan and stir to mix well. Let stand 5 minutes.

2. Cook the milk mixture over medium heat, stirring constantly, until the mixture comes to a boil, about 6 minutes. Remove from the heat and stir in the vanilla. Transfer the pudding to a medium bowl and place a sheet of wax paper on the surface of the pudding to prevent a skin from forming. Cool to room temperature. Stir the pudding and refrigerate, covered, until chilled, 4 hours or overnight.

Nutrition Info:

31 g carb, 173 cal, 2 g fat, 1 g sat fat, 59 mg chol, 0 g fib, 6 g pro, 144 mg sod •
Carb Choices: 2; Exchanges: 2 carb

Microwave Corn-on-the-cob

Servings: 2

Ingredients:

2 ears corn with husks

1 teaspoon butter

1⁄8 teaspoon salt

Directions:

1. Place the corn with the husks intact in the microwave and cook on high 5 minutes.

2. Carefully remove from the microwave using tongs or an oven mitt, place under cold running water, and remove the husks. The corn will cool, but just enough to be ready to eat immediately.

3. Rub each ear with 1/2 teaspoon of the butter and sprinkle evenly with the salt. Serve at once.

Nutrition Info:

17 g carb, 94 cal, 3 g fat, 1 g sat fat, 5 mg chol, 2 g fib, 3 g pro, 159 mg sod • Carb Choices: 1; Exchanges: 1 starch, 1/2 fat

Ginger-plum Crostata

Servings: 12

Ingredients:

1 recipe Pastry Crust

1 1/4 pounds plums, pitted and sliced

1/4 cup plus 2 teaspoons sugar, divided

1/4 cup unbleached all-purpose flour

2 tablespoons minced crystallized ginger

2 teaspoons unsalted butter, melted

Directions:

1. Preheat the oven to 400°F.

2. Place the pastry dough between two sheets of parchment paper. Roll the dough into a 12-inch circle. Set aside, leaving the dough between the parchment paper to prevent it from drying out.

3. Combine the plums, 1/4 cup of the sugar, the flour, and ginger in a large bowl and toss to coat. Transfer the dough inside the parchment paper sheets onto a large baking sheet. Remove the top layer of parchment.

4. Mound the plum mixture in the center of the dough. Carefully fold the dough up and over the edge of the filling, pleating as necessary. Brush the dough with the melted butter and sprinkle with the remaining 2 teaspoons sugar. Bake until the plums are bubbly and the crust is browned, 30 to 35 minutes. Serve warm or at room temperature. The crostata is best the day it is made.

Nutrition Info:

27 g carb, 165 cal, 6 g fat, 3 g sat fat, 14 mg chol, 3 g fib, 2 g pro, 59 mg sod • Carb Choices: 2; Exchanges: 1 1/2 carb, 1/2 fruit, 1 fat

Asian Beef Lettuce Wraps

Servings: 4

Ingredients:

1 pound 95% lean ground beef

2 tablespoons minced fresh ginger

3 tablespoons reduced-sodium soy sauce

1 tablespoon lime juice

1/4 teaspoon Asian sesame oil

1/4 teaspoon chili-garlic paste

1/2 cup thinly sliced scallions

2 tablespoons chopped fresh mint

2 tablespoons chopped fresh cilantro

1 small head Bibb lettuce, separated into leaves

1 hothouse (English) cucumber, cut into short, thin strips

1 cup bean sprouts

Lime wedges

Directions:

1. Combine the beef and ginger in a medium nonstick skillet. Place over medium-high heat and cook, stirring occasionally, until the beef is browned, about 8 minutes. Stir in the soy sauce, lime juice, oil, and chili-garlic paste and cook, stirring often, until most of the liquid has evaporated, about 2 minutes.

2. To serve, transfer the beef mixture to a serving bowl and stir in the scallions, mint, and cilantro. Arrange the lettuce, cucumber, and bean sprouts on a serving platter. Allow each person to assemble their own rolls, spooning the beef into the lettuce leaves and topping with the cucumber and bean sprouts. Serve with the lime wedges.

Nutrition Info:

7 g carb, 195 cal, 7 g fat, 3 g sat fat, 67 mg chol, 2 g fib, 27 g pro, 535 mg sod • Carb Choices: 1/2; Exchanges: 1 veg, 3 lean protein

Classic Chocolate Chippers

Servings: 36

Ingredients:

1/2 cup unbleached all-purpose flour

1/2 cup whole wheat flour

1/4 teaspoon baking soda

1/4 teaspoon salt

4 tablespoons (1/2 stick) unsalted butter, softened

1/2 cup granulated sugar

1/2 cup packed light brown sugar

1 large egg

1 teaspoon vanilla extract

1/2 cup semisweet chocolate chips

Directions:

1. Preheat the oven to 350°F. Line 2 baking sheets with parchment paper.

2. Combine the all-purpose flour, whole wheat flour, baking soda, and salt in a medium bowl and whisk to mix well.

3. Place the butter in a large bowl and beat at medium speed with an electric mixer until fluffy. Gradually beat in the sugars. Beat in the egg and vanilla. Add the flour mixture and beat at low speed just until blended. Stir in the chocolate chips.

4. Drop the batter by level tablespoonfuls 2 inches apart onto the prepared baking sheets. Bake until the edges of the cookies are lightly browned, 10 to 12 minutes. Cool the cookies on the baking sheets for 2 minutes. Transfer to wire racks to cool completely. The cookies can be stored in an airtight container at room temperature for up to 3 days.

Nutrition Info:

10 g carb, 63 cal, 2 g fat, 1 g sat fat, 9 mg chol, 0 g fib, 1 g pro, 28 mg sod • Carb Choices: 1/2; Exchanges: 1/2 carb, 1/2 fat

Roasted Zucchini with Toasted Cumin And Basil

Servings: 4

Ingredients:

2 medium zucchinis

2 teaspoons plus 1 tablespoon extra virgin olive oil, divided

1/2 teaspoon kosher salt, divided

1/4 teaspoon cumin seeds

1/2 teaspoon grated lemon zest

2 teaspoons lemon juice

Pinch of freshly ground pepper

1 tablespoon chopped fresh basil

Directions:

1. Preheat the oven to 425°F.

2. Halve the zucchini crosswise and cut each half into quarters lengthwise. Place on a large rimmed baking sheet. Drizzle with 2 teaspoons of the oil and sprinkle with ¼ teaspoon of the salt. Toss to coat. Arrange in a single layer.

3. Roast, turning the zucchini once, until tender and browned, 25 to 30 minutes.

4. Meanwhile, place the cumin in a small dry skillet over medium heat and toast, shaking the pan often, until the cumin is fragrant, about 3 minutes. Transfer to a small plate and allow to cool. Place the cumin in a mortar and crush with a pestle. Alternatively, place the cumin in a small resealable plastic bag. Seal the bag, place on a cutting board, and crush using a meat mallet or the back of a large spoon.

5. Place the cumin in a small bowl. Add the lemon zest, lemon juice, the remaining ¼ teaspoon salt, and the pepper and whisk to combine. Slowly whisk in the remaining 1 tablespoon oil.

6. Arrange the zucchini on a platter, drizzle with the oil mixture, and sprinkle with the basil. Serve hot, warm, or at room temperature.

Nutrition Info:

4 g carb, 70 cal, 6 g fat, 1 g sat fat, 0 mg chol, 1 g fib, 1 g pro, 151 mg sod • Carb Choices: 0; Exchanges: 1 veg, 1 fat

Strawberry Pie

Servings: 12

Ingredients:

8 cups halved (or quartered if large) fresh strawberries

1/4 cup sugar

3 tablespoons cornstarch

1/2 cup water

1 tablespoon lemon juice

1 recipe Graham Cracker Crust

12 tablespoons Light Whipped Cream

Directions:

1. Place 6 cups of the strawberries in a large bowl and set aside. Place the remaining 2 cups berries in a food processor and process until smooth.

2. Combine the pureed strawberries, sugar, cornstarch, and water in a medium saucepan and whisk until smooth. Cook over medium-high heat, stirring constantly, until the mixture comes to a boil and thickens, about 5 minutes. Remove from the heat and stir in the lemon juice.

3. Pour the hot mixture over the strawberries. Working quickly, toss the berries to coat and transfer into the prepared crust. Refrigerate until set, about 3 hours. The pie is best on the day it is made. Top each slice with 1 tablespoon of the whipped cream.

Nutrition Info:

26 g carb, 152 cal, 5 g fat, 2 g sat fat, 12 mg chol, 3 g fib, 3 g pro, 82 mg sod • Carb Choices: 2; Exchanges: 1 1/2 carb, 1/2 fruit, 1 fat

Potato-cauliflower Mash

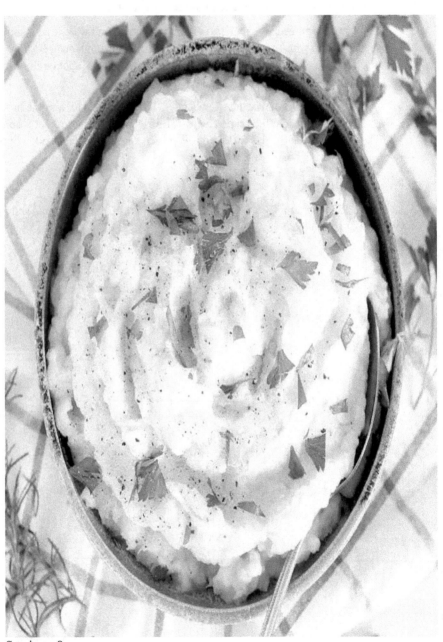

Servings: 8

Ingredients:

1 pound Yukon Gold or baking potatoes, peeled and cut into 1-inch chunks

1 pound cauliflower, cut into 1-inch florets (about 4 cups)

1/3 cup plain low-fat yogurt

1/2 teaspoon kosher salt

1/8 teaspoon freshly ground pepper

Directions:

1. Place the potatoes and cauliflower in a large saucepan. Add water to cover and bring to a boil over high heat. Cover, reduce the heat to low, and simmer until the vegetables are fork-tender, about 15 minutes.

2. Drain the vegetables in a colander and return to the pan. Add the yogurt, salt, and pepper and mash with a potato masher to the desired consistency. Spoon the potatoes into a serving dish and serve at once.

Nutrition Info:

11 g carb, 53 cal, 0 g fat, 0 g sat fat, 1 mg chol, 1 g fib, 2 g pro, 86 mg sod • Carb Choices: 1; Exchanges: 1 starch

Bread Salad

Servings: 8

Ingredients:

4 ounces whole grain bread, cut into 1/2-inch cubes (about 21/2 cups)

4 cups loosely packed torn romaine lettuce

1 large tomato, chopped

1 large hothouse (English) cucumber, halved lengthwise and sliced

1/2 cup red Roasted Bell Peppers or roasted red peppers from a jar, thinly sliced

1/4 cup thinly sliced red onion

1 recipe Basic Vinaigrette

1 ounce finely shredded Parmesan (about 1/4 cup)

Directions:

1. Preheat the oven to 350°F. Place the bread cubes in a single layer on a large rimmed baking sheet. Bake, stirring once, until lightly toasted, 8 minutes. Let cool to room temperature.

2. Combine the toasted bread cubes, lettuce, tomato, cucumber, roasted peppers, and onion in a large bowl. Drizzle with the vinaigrette and toss to coat. Divide the salad among 8 plates and sprinkle evenly with the Parmesan. Serve at once.

Nutrition Info:

10 g carb, 107 cal, 7 g fat, 1 g sat fat, 3 mg chol, 3 g fib, 3 g pro, 141 mg sod • Carb Choices: 1/2; Exchanges: 1/2 carb, 1 fat

Autumn Greens Tart

Servings: 6

Ingredients:

1 Pastry Crust, prepared without sugar

2 teaspoons extra virgin olive oil

1 small onion, chopped

2 garlic cloves, minced

1/2 cup water

8 ounces kale, tough stems removed and leaves chopped

8 ounces Swiss chard, tough stems removed and leaves chopped

1 cup low-fat cottage cheese

1/3 cup freshly grated Parmesan

2 large egg whites

1 large egg

1/2 teaspoon kosher salt

1/8 teaspoon crushed red pepper

Directions:

1. Preheat the oven to 400°F.

2. Place the pastry dough between two sheets of wax paper. Roll the dough into a 12-inch circle. Remove the top layer of wax paper and place the dough, with the remaining sheet of wax paper facing up, into a 9-inch tart pan with a removable bottom. Trim the edge of the crust to fit the pan. Prick the bottom of the crust all over with a fork. Line the crust with parchment paper and fill with pie weights or dried beans. Place the tart pan on a rimmed baking sheet and bake 20 minutes. Remove the parchment and weights and bake until the crust is lightly browned, 5 to 8 minutes. Maintain the oven temperature.

3. Meanwhile, heat a large nonstick skillet over medium heat. Add the oil and tilt the pan to coat the bottom evenly. Add the onion and cook, stirring often, until softened, 5 minutes. Add the garlic and cook, stirring constantly, until fragrant, 30 seconds.

4. Add the water, then add the kale and chard in batches and cook, stirring constantly, until wilted. Cover and cook, stirring frequently, until the greens are tender, 6 to 8 minutes. Transfer to a colander and let stand until cool enough to handle. Squeeze the greens mixture dry.

5. Combine the greens mixture, cottage cheese, Parmesan, egg whites, egg, salt, and crushed red pepper in a large bowl and add to the stir to mix well.

6. Spoon the greens mixture into the prepared crust, spreading evenly. Place the tart pan on a large rimmed baking sheet and bake until the tart is set, 25 to 28 minutes. Let stand 5 minutes before slicing. Cut into 6 wedges and serve hot, warm, or at room temperature.

Nutrition Info:

25 g carb, 259 cal, 12 g fat, 6 g sat fat, 61 mg chol, 4 g fib, 13 g pro, 527 mg sod • Carb Choices: 1 1/2; Exchanges: 1 1/2 starch, 1 veg, 2 fat

Shortbread

Servings: 16

Ingredients:

1 teaspoon plus 1/2 cup (1 stick) unsalted butter, softened, divided

2 cups unbleached all-purpose flour

1/4 cup cornstarch

1/4 teaspoon salt

1/2 cup canola oil

1/2 cup sugar

2 teaspoons vanilla extract

Directions:

1. Preheat the oven to 350°F. Line an 8-inch square metal baking pan with foil, allowing the foil to extend over the rim of the pan by 2 inches. Brush the foil with 1 teaspoon of the butter.

2. Combine the flour, cornstarch, and salt in a medium bowl and whisk to mix well.

3. Place the remaining 1/2 cup butter in a large bowl and beat at medium speed with an electric mixer until fluffy. with the mixer running, slowly beat in the oil. Gradually beat in the sugar. Beat in the vanilla. Add the flour mixture and beat at low speed just until well mixed.

4. Spread the dough evenly into the prepared pan. Bake until the edges of the shortbread are lightly browned, 25 to 30 minutes (do not overbake). Cool in the pan on a wire rack for 5 minutes, then cut the shortbread into 24 squares in the pan. Cool the shortbread completely in the pan on a wire rack. The shortbread can be stored in an airtight container at room temperature for up to 1 week.

Nutrition Info:

13 g carb, 136 cal, 9 g fat, 3 g sat fat, 10 mg chol, 0 g fib, 1 g pro, 25 mg sod • Carb choices: 1; Exchanges: 1 carb, 1 1/2 fat

Chicken Simmered with Fennel And Tomatoes

Servings: 4

Ingredients:

4 (6-ounce) bone-in chicken breast halves, skinned

1/2 teaspoon kosher salt, divided

1/4 teaspoon freshly ground pepper, divided

2 tablespoons unbleached all-purpose flour

4 teaspoons extra virgin olive oil, divided

1 medium fennel bulb, tough outer leaves removed, cored and thinly sliced

1 small onion, halved lengthwise and thinly sliced

1 garlic clove, minced

1 1/2 cups Chicken Stock or low-sodium chicken broth

1 tablespoon Dijon mustard

1 cup cherry tomatoes, halved

2 tablespoons chopped fresh Italian parsley

Directions:

1. Sprinkle the chicken with 1/4 teaspoon of the salt and 1/8 teaspoon of the pepper, then with the flour. Heat a large deep skillet over medium heat. Add 2 teaspoons of the oil and tilt the pan to coat the bottom evenly. Add the chicken and cook, turning often, until well browned on both sides, about 8 minutes. Transfer to a plate.

2. Add the remaining 2 teaspoons oil to the skillet and tilt the pan to coat the bottom evenly. Add the fennel and onion to the skillet and cook, stirring often, until softened, 5 minutes. Add the garlic and cook, stirring constantly until fragrant, 30 seconds. Add the stock, mustard, remaining 1/4 teaspoon salt, and remaining 1/8 teaspoon pepper and stir to combine. Return the chicken to the skillet and bring to a boil. Cover, reduce the heat to low, and simmer until the juices of the chicken run clear, about 30 minutes. Add the tomatoes and cook just until heated through, 1 minute. Stir in the parsley. Divide the chicken among 4 plates. Spoon the vegetables and cooking liquid over the chicken and serve at once.

Nutrition Info:

11 g carb, 240 cal, 8 g fat, 2 g sat fat, 72 mg chol, 3 g fib, 30 g pro, 374 mg sod • Carb Choices: 1; Exchanges: 1/2 starch, 2 veg, 3 lean protein, 1 fat

Beef Pot Roast with Root Vegetables

Servings: 6

Ingredients:

2 pounds beef chuck shoulder roast or bottom round roast, trimmed of all visible fat

1 teaspoon kosher salt

1/2 teaspoon freshly ground pepper

4 teaspoons extra virgin olive oil, divided

2 carrots, peeled and chopped

2 stalks celery, chopped

1 medium onion, chopped

4 garlic cloves, chopped

2 to 3 cups Beef Stock or low-sodium beef broth, divided

1/4 cup no-salt-added tomato paste

1 pound red-skinned potatoes, well scrubbed and cut into 1-inch pieces

8 ounces parsnips, peeled and cut into 1-inch pieces

8 ounces turnips, peeled and cut into 1-inch pieces

Directions:

1. Preheat the oven to 325°F.

2. Sprinkle the roast with the salt and pepper. Heat a Dutch oven over medium-high heat. Add 2 teaspoons of the oil and tilt the pan to coat the bottom evenly. Add the roast and cook, turning to brown on all sides, 6 to 8 minutes. Transfer the roast to a plate.

3. Add the remaining 2 teaspoons oil to the Dutch oven and tilt to coat. Add the carrots, celery, and onion and cook, stirring often, until the vegetables are softened, 5 minutes. Add the garlic and cook, stirring constantly, 30 seconds. Add 2 cups of the stock and bring to a boil, stirring to scrape up the browned bits from the bottom of the Dutch oven. Return the roast to the Dutch oven. Add the tomato paste and bring to a boil. Add the additional stock, if necessary, to almost cover the roast. Cover and bake 2 hours.

4. Remove the Dutch oven from the oven and arrange the potatoes, parsnips, and turnips around the roast (add additional stock or water, if necessary to almost cover the vegetables). Cover and bake until the roast and the vegetables are very tender, about 1 hour longer.

5. Remove the roast from the Dutch oven, place on a serving platter, and cover with foil.

6. Pour the vegetable mixture through a strainer and transfer the vegetables to the platter with the roast. Pour the strained broth into a medium saucepan and bring to a boil over high heat. Cook, uncovered, until reduced to about 1 1/2 cups, about 8 minutes. Cut the roast into thick slices and divide the roast and vegetables evenly among 6 shallow bowls. Ladle the broth evenly over the beef and vegetables and serve at once.

Nutrition Info:

20 g carb, 255 cal, 8 g fat, 2 g sat fat, 49 mg chol, 4 g fib, 24 g pro, 213 mg sod • Carb Choices: 1; Exchanges: 1 starch, 1 veg, 3 lean protein, 1/2 fat

Lemony Bulgur Pilaf with Kalamata Olives

Servings: 6

Ingredients:

2 teaspoons extra virgin olive oil

1/2 cup diced onion

1 garlic clove, minced

2 cups Vegetable Stock or low-sodium vegetable broth

3/4 cup medium- or coarse-grind bulgur

1/4 teaspoon kosher salt

Pinch of freshly ground pepper

3 tablespoons Kalamata olives, pitted and sliced

2 tablespoons chopped fresh Italian parsley

2 teaspoons grated lemon zest

1 tablespoon lemon juice

Directions:

1. Heat a medium nonstick skillet over medium heat. Add the oil and tilt the pan to coat the bottom evenly. Add the onion and cook, stirring often, until softened, 5 minutes. Add the garlic and cook, stirring constantly, until fragrant, 30 seconds.

2. Stir in the stock, bulgur, salt, and pepper and bring to a boil over high heat. Cover, reduce the heat to low, and simmer until the liquid has absorbed and bulgur is tender, 15 to 18 minutes.

3. Remove from the heat and stir in the olives, parsley, lemon zest, and lemon juice. Spoon the pilaf into a serving dish and serve at once.

Nutrition Info:

17 g carb, 103 cal, 3 g fat, 0 g sat fat, 0 mg chol, 4 g fib, 2 g pro, 174 mg sod • Carb Choices: 1; Exchanges: 1 starch, 1/2 fat

Curried Stuffed Eggs

Servings: 8

Ingredients:

12 large eggs

2 tablespoons mayonnaise

2 tablespoons plain low-fat yogurt

2 tablespoons finely minced mango chutney

1 teaspoon white wine vinegar

1 teaspoon curry powder

1/4 teaspoon kosher salt

2 tablespoons minced red onion

2 tablespoons minced celery

1 tablespoon chopped fresh Italian parsley

Directions:

1. Place the eggs in a large saucepan and cover with cold water. Cover and bring to a boil over medium heat. Turn off the heat and let the eggs stand 12 minutes. Drain and peel under cold running water.

2. Cut the eggs in half lengthwise. Remove and discard 6 of the egg yolks. Combine the remaining egg yolks, the mayonnaise, yogurt, chutney, vinegar, curry powder, and salt and stir until smooth, breaking up the egg yolks with a spatula or fork.

3. Finely chop 8 of the egg white halves and add to the egg yolk mixture. Stir in the onion, celery, and parsley. Spoon the egg yolk mixture evenly into the remaining 16 egg white halves. Arrange on a serving plate. Cover and refrigerate until chilled, at least 2 hours and up to 1 day.

Nutrition Info:

4 g carb, 104 cal, 6 g fat, 2 g sat fat, 155 mg chol, 0 g fib, 8 g pro, 157 mg sod •
Carb Choices: 0; Exchanges: 1 lean protein, 1/2 fat

Tuna And White Bean Salad with Spinach

Servings: 4

Ingredients:

2 (5-ounce) cans low-sodium chunk white albacore tuna in water, drained and flaked

1 (15-ounce) can no-salt-added cannellini or navy beans, rinsed and drained

1 cup chopped hothouse (English) cucumber

1/4 cup diced red onion

2 tablespoons chopped fresh Italian parsley

1 tablespoon capers, rinsed and drained

4 tablespoons Lemon Vinaigrette, divided

6 cups loosely packed fresh baby spinach

4 plum tomatoes, quartered

Directions:

1. Combine the tuna, beans, cucumber, onion, parsley, and capers in a medium bowl. Drizzle with 2 tablespoons of the vinaigrette and toss to coat. The salad can be made up to this point and refrigerated, covered, for up to 2 days.

2. Place the spinach in a large bowl. Drizzle with the remaining vinaigrette and toss to coat. Divide the spinach evenly among 4 plates. Top evenly with the tuna mixture and top evenly with the tomatoes. Serve at once.

Nutrition Info:

27 g carb, 268 cal, 10 g fat, 1 g sat fat, 25 mg chol, 10 g fib, 21 g pro, 267 mg sod • Carb Choices: 1 1/2; Exchanges: 1 starch, 2 veg, 2 lean protein, 1 1/2 fat

Spicy Eggplant with Ginger And Sesame

Servings: 4

Ingredients:

1 (1-pound) eggplant, peeled and cut into 1/2-inch cubes

2 teaspoons reduced-sodium soy sauce

1 teaspoon rice vinegar

1/2 teaspoon chili-garlic paste

1/8 teaspoon Asian sesame oil

2 teaspoons canola oil

1 tablespoon minced fresh ginger

2 garlic cloves, minced

1/4 teaspoon kosher salt

1 small scallion, thinly sliced

Directions:

1. In a pot fitted with a steamer basket, bring 1 inch of water to a boil over high heat. Add the eggplant cubes, reduce heat to low, cover, and steam until tender but still retain their shape, about 5 minutes. Transfer to a colander and drain.
2. Meanwhile, stir together the soy sauce, vinegar, chili-garlic paste, and sesame oil in a small dish. Set aside.
3. Heat a large nonstick skillet over medium-high heat. Add the canola oil and tilt the pan to coat the bottom evenly. Add the ginger and garlic and cook, stirring constantly, until fragrant, 30 seconds. Add the eggplant, sprinkle with the salt, and stir to coat. Remove from the heat and stir in the soy sauce mixture.
4. Spoon into a serving bowl and sprinkle with the scallion. Serve at once.

Nutrition Info:

6 g carb, 49 cal, 3 g fat, 3 g sat fat, 0 mg chol, 3 g fib, 1 g pro, 200 mg sod • Carb Choices: 1/2; Exchanges: 1 veg, 1/2 fat

Shrimp Bruschetta

Servings: 8

Ingredients:

1 tablespoon mayonnaise

1 tablespoon plain low-fat yogurt

1 teaspoon grated lemon zest

1 tablespoon lemon juice

1/2 teaspoon ground coriander

1/4 teaspoon kosher salt

6 ounces cooked peeled deveined shrimp, chopped

2 tablespoons minced red or yellow bell pepper

2 tablespoons chopped fresh Italian parsley

1 tablespoon minced scallions, green tops only

16 (1/4-inch) slices whole wheat baguette, toasted

Directions:

1. Stir together the mayonnaise, yogurt, lemon zest, lemon juice, coriander, and salt in a medium bowl. Add the shrimp, bell pepper, parsley, and scallions.

2. To assemble, spoon about 1 tablespoon of the shrimp mixture on each of the baguette slices. Arrange on a platter and serve at once.

Nutrition Info:

13 g carb, 117 cal, 3 g fat, 0 g sat fat, 44 mg chol, 2 g fib, 10 g pro, 253 mg sod • Carb Choices: 1; Exchanges: 1 starch, 1 lean protein, 1/2 fat

Pears Poached In Vanilla-anise Syrup

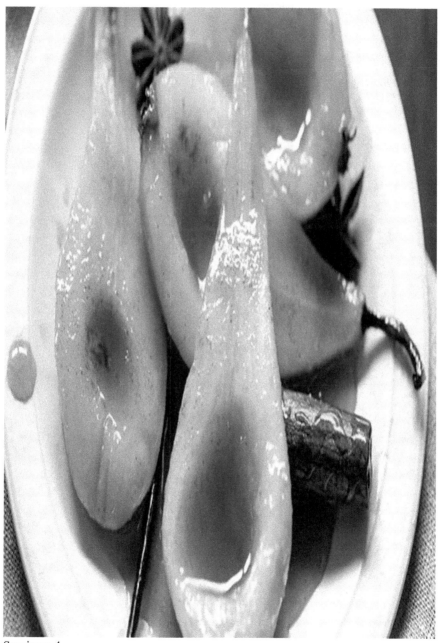

Servings: 4

Ingredients:

4 medium Bosc pears

2 cups Riesling or Gewürztraminer

3 tablespoons sugar

1/2 vanilla bean, split

2 whole star anise

Directions:

1. Peel the pears, leaving the stems intact. If necessary, cut a thin slice off the bottom of each pear so they will sit upright.

2. Combine the Riesling, sugar, vanilla bean, and star anise in a large saucepan or Dutch oven and bring to a boil over high heat. Carefully place the pears in the saucepan. Reduce the heat to low, cover, and simmer until the pears are tender when pierced with a knife, 10 to 15 minutes. Transfer the pears to a plate with a slotted spoon and cool to room temperature.

3. Meanwhile, increase the heat to medium-high and boil the cooking liquid, uncovered, until reduced to about 1 cup, 15 to 20 minutes. Remove and discard the vanilla bean and star anise. Serve the pears with the syrup at room temperature or chilled.

Nutrition Info:

39 g carb, 232 cal, 1 g fat, 0 g sat fat, 0 mg chol, 1 g fib, 1 g pro, 0 mg sod • Carb Choices: 2 1/2; Exchanges: 1 carb, 1 1/2 fruit

Asian Cucumber Salad

Servings: 4

Ingredients:

1 large hothouse (English) cucumber, thinly sliced

2 tablespoons rice vinegar

2 scallions, thinly sliced

2 tablespoons chopped fresh cilantro

1/2 teaspoon kosher salt

1/4 teaspoon Asian sesame oil

1 teaspoon toasted sesame seeds

Directions:

1. Combine the cucumber and vinegar in a medium shallow dish. Refrigerate, covered, stirring occasionally, until chilled, at least 2 hours and up to 12 hours.

2. To serve, add the scallions, cilantro, salt, and oil and toss to combine. Sprinkle with the sesame seeds and serve at once.

Nutrition Info:

4 g carb, 25 cal, 1 g fat, 0 g sat fat, 0 mg chol, 1 g fib, 1 g pro, 143 mg sod • Carb Choices: 0; Exchanges: 1 veg

Roasted Garlic Mashed Potatoes

Servings: 4

Ingredients:

6 garlic cloves, unpeeled

1 pound Yukon Gold or baking potatoes, peeled and cut into 1-inch chunks

1 cup low-sodium vegetable or chicken broth

1/4 cup plain low-fat yogurt

2 teaspoons unsalted butter

1/2 teaspoon kosher salt

Pinch of freshly ground pepper

Directions:

1. Preheat the oven to 350°F.

2. Wrap the garlic cloves in a sheet of foil and place in a small baking dish. Bake until the garlic is very soft, about 30 minutes. Unwrap the garlic and let stand until cool enough to handle. Squeeze the garlic pulp from each clove into a small bowl.

3. Meanwhile, place the potatoes and broth in a large saucepan and bring to a boil over high heat. Cover, reduce the heat to low, and simmer until the potatoes are fork-tender, about 15 minutes.

4. Drain the potatoes in a colander and return to the pan. Add the garlic pulp, the yogurt, butter, salt, and pepper. Mash the potatoes with a potato masher to the desired consistency. Spoon the potatoes into a serving dish and serve at once.

Nutrition Info:

23 g carb, 121 cal, 2 g fat, 1 g sat fat, 6 mg chol, 2 g fib, 3 g pro, 276 mg sod • Carb Choices: 1 1/2; Exchanges: 1 1/2 starch, 1/2 fat

Arugula And Melon Salad with Crispy Prosciutto

Servings: 4

Ingredients:

4 ounces prosciutto, trimmed of all visible fat, cut into thin strips

2 tablespoons rice vinegar

1 tablespoon extra virgin olive oil

1/2 teaspoon honey

1/4 teaspoon kosher salt

Pinch of freshly ground pepper

6 cups loosely packed arugula

1/4 medium honeydew melon, seeded, peeled, and thinly sliced

1/4 medium cantaloupe, seeded, peeled, and thinly sliced

Directions:

1. Preheat the oven to 400°F.

2. Line a medium rimmed baking sheet with parchment paper. Place the prosciutto in the pan and bake until lightly browned, 8 to 10 minutes. Transfer the prosciutto to a paper towel–lined plate to cool.

3. Meanwhile, whisk together the vinegar, oil, honey, salt, and pepper in a large bowl. Add the arugula and toss to coat. Divide the salad evenly among 4 plates. Top evenly with the honeydew and cantaloupe and sprinkle evenly with the prosciutto. Serve at once.

Nutrition Info:

13 g carb, 148 cal, 7 g fat, 2 g sat fat, 25 mg chol, 2 g fib, 9 g pro, 646 mg sod • Carb Choices: 1; Exchanges: 1 fruit, 1 medium-fat protein, 1 fat

Pork And Hominy Soup

Servings: 6

Ingredients:

8 ounces boneless center-cut pork chops, trimmed of all visible fat and cubed

2 teaspoons canola oil

1 medium onion, chopped

1 small green bell pepper, chopped

2 garlic cloves, minced

2 tablespoons chili powder

1 tablespoon ground cumin

1/4 teaspoon freshly ground pepper

3 cups Chicken Stock or low-sodium chicken broth

1 (141/2-ounce) can no-salt-added diced tomatoes

1 (15-ounce) can hominy, rinsed and drained

1 tablespoon fine-grind yellow cornmeal

Chopped fresh cilantro

Lime wedges

Directions:

1. Place the pork in a food processor in 2 batches and pulse until the meat is finely minced but not ground, 4 to 5 times.

2. Heat a large pot over medium heat. Add the oil and tilt the pan to coat the bottom evenly. Add the pork, onion, and bell pepper and cook, stirring often, until the vegetables are softened, 8 minutes. Add the garlic, chili powder, cumin, and ground pepper and cook, stirring constantly, until fragrant, 30 seconds.

3. Stir in the stock, tomatoes, and hominy and bring to a boil over high heat. Cover, reduce the heat to low, and simmer until the vegetables are tender, about 15 minutes. Sprinkle the cornmeal into the soup, stirring constantly. Simmer until slightly thickened, about 2 minutes. Ladle the soup into 6 bowls, sprinkle with the cilantro, and serve at once with lime wedges on the side. The soup can be refrigerated, covered, for up to 4 days or frozen for up to 3 months.

Nutrition Info:

16 g carb, 157 cal, 5 g fat, 1 g sat fat, 25 mg chol, 3 g fib, 12 g pro, 275 mg sod •
Carb Choices: 1; Exchanges: 1/2 starch, 1 veg, 1 lean protein

Broccoli Rabe with Garlic And Sun-dried Tomatoes

Servings: 2

Ingredients:

1 pound broccoli rabe, tough stems removed, leaves and florets chopped

2 teaspoons extra virgin olive oil

4 garlic cloves, thinly sliced

1/4 cup Chicken Stock or low-sodium chicken broth

4 dry-packed sun-dried tomatoes, thinly sliced

1/2 teaspoon kosher salt

1/8 teaspoon crushed red pepper

2 tablespoons freshly grated Parmesan

Directions:

1. Bring a large pot of water to a boil over high heat. Add the broccoli rabe and cook until barely tender, 5 minutes. Drain in a colander.

2. Meanwhile, heat a large nonstick skillet over medium heat. Add the oil and tilt the pan to coat the bottom evenly. Add the garlic and cook, stirring often, until lightly browned, 3 minutes. Add the broccoli rabe, stock, tomatoes, salt, and crushed red pepper. Cook, stirring occasionally, until the broccoli rabe is very tender and the liquid evaporates, about 5 minutes. Spoon the broccoli rabe into a serving bowl and sprinkle with the Parmesan.

Nutrition Info:

8 g carb, 113 cal, 7 g fat, 2 g sat fat, 5 mg chol, 4 g fib, 7 g pro, 358 mg sod • Carb Choices: 1/2; Exchanges: 1 veg, 1 1/2 fat

Pumpkin Pie

Servings: 12

Ingredients:

1 recipe Pastry Crust

1 (15-ounce) can pumpkin (not pumpkin pie filling)

1/2 cup fat-free evaporated milk

3/4 cup packed light brown sugar

2 large eggs

1 teaspoon vanilla extract

1/2 teaspoon ground cinnamon

1/4 teaspoon allspice

1/8 teaspoon cloves

Directions:

1.   Preheat the oven to 425°F.

2.   Place the pastry dough between two sheets of wax paper. Roll the dough into a 12-inch circle. Remove the top layer of wax paper and place the dough, with the wax paper facing up, into a 9-inch glass pie plate. Starting from the edge of the dough, gently remove the wax paper. Fold the overhanging dough under and crimp the edge decoratively.

3.   Combine the pumpkin, milk, sugar, eggs, vanilla, cinnamon, allspice, and cloves in a large bowl and whisk until smooth. Pour into the prepared crust.

4.   Bake 15 minutes. Reduce the oven temperature to 350°F and bake until the filling is set, 35 to 40 minutes. Cover the edge of the crust with foil, if necessary, to prevent overbrowning. Cool completely on a wire rack before serving. The pie is best on the day it is made.

Nutrition Info:

28 g carb, 168 cal, 5 g fat, 3 g sat fat, 45 mg chol, 2 g fib, 3 g pro, 81 mg sod • Carb Choices: 2; Exchanges: 2 carb, 1 fat

Grilled Shrimp with Thai Slaw

Servings: 4

Ingredients:

1/3 cup lime juice

1/4 cup Asian fish sauce

2 tablespoons cold water

1 tablespoon plus 1/2 teaspoon canola oil, divided

1 teaspoon chili-garlic paste

1 tablespoon sugar

1 pound large peeled and deveined shrimp

3 cups thinly sliced savoy or napa cabbage

2 scallions, thinly sliced

1 small zucchini, cut into thin strips (about 1 cup)

1 small red bell pepper, cut into thin strips (about 1 cup)

1 small carrot, peeled and coarsely shredded

1 jalapeño, seeded and minced

1/2 hothouse (English) cucumber, seeded and cut into thin strips (about 1/2 cup)

1/4 cup chopped fresh cilantro

1/4 cup chopped fresh mint

Directions:

1. Combine the lime juice, fish sauce, water, 1 tablespoon of the oil, the chili-garlic paste, and sugar in a large bowl and stir until the sugar dissolves. Transfer 1/3 cup of the lime juice mixture to a shallow dish. Add the shrimp and toss to coat. Cover and refrigerate 30 minutes.

2. Meanwhile, combine the cabbage, scallions, zucchini, bell pepper, carrot, jalapeño, cucumber, cilantro, and mint in a large bowl. Cover and refrigerate until ready to serve. Just before serving, drizzle the vegetables with the remaining lime juice mixture and toss to coat.

3. Preheat the grill to medium-high heat.

4. Brush the grill rack with the remaining 1/2 teaspoon oil. Remove the shrimp from the marinade and discard the marinade. Place the shrimp on the grill and grill, turning once, just until the shrimp turn pink, about 4 minutes. Divide the shrimp and slaw among 4 plates and serve at once.

Nutrition Info:

12 g carb, 153 cal, 3 g fat, 0 g sat fat, 168 mg chol, 3 g fib, 20 g pro, 940 mg sod •
Carb Choices: 1; Exchanges: 2 veg, 3 lean protein

Bibb And Whole Herb Salad

Servings: 4

Ingredients:

2 tablespoons lemon juice

1 1/2 tablespoons extra virgin olive oil

1/4 teaspoon kosher salt

1/8 teaspoon freshly ground pepper

8 cups loosely packed torn Bibb lettuce

1/2 cup loosely packed fresh Italian parsley leaves

1/2 cup loosely packed fresh basil leaves, thinly sliced if large

1/4 cup loosely packed small fresh dill sprigs

Directions:

1. Whisk together the lemon juice, oil, salt, and pepper in a large bowl.

2. Add the lettuce, parsley, basil, and dill and toss to coat. Divide the salad among 4 plates. Serve at once.

Nutrition Info:

4 g carb, 68 cal, 6 g fat, 1 g sat fat, 0 mg chol, 2 g fib, 2 g pro, 80 mg sod • Carb Choices: 0; Exchanges: 1 veg, 1 fat

Mediterranean Bean Salad with Artichokes And Lemon

Servings: 4

Ingredients:

1 (14-ounce) can artichoke hearts

1 teaspoon grated lemon zest

2 tablespoons lemon juice

1 1/2 tablespoon extra virgin olive oil

1 garlic clove, minced

1 teaspoon Dijon mustard

1/4 teaspoon kosher salt

1/8 teaspoon freshly ground pepper

1 (15-ounce) can no-salt-added cannellini beans, rinsed and drained

1/2 cup red Roasted Bell Peppers or roasted red peppers from a jar, chopped

1/4 cup thinly sliced red onion

2 teaspoons chopped fresh rosemary or 1 tablespoon chopped fresh Italian parsley

Directions:

1. Drain the artichokes and cut into quarters. Place the artichokes on several thicknesses of paper towels and gently blot dry. Set aside.

2. Whisk together the lemon zest, lemon juice, oil, garlic, mustard, salt, and ground pepper in a large bowl. Add the artichokes, beans, roasted peppers, onion, and rosemary and toss gently to coat. Serve the salad at room temperature. The salad tastes best on the day it is made, but it can be refrigerated, covered, for up to 1 day. Let stand at room temperature 30 minutes before serving.

Nutrition Info:

23 g carb, 180 cal, 6 g fat, 1 g sat fat, 0 mg chol, 5 g fib, 8 g pro, 355 mg sod • Carb Choices: 11/2; Exchanges: 1 starch, 1 veg, 1 plant- based protein, 1 fat

Meringue Cookies

Servings: 18

Ingredients:

3 large egg whites

1/4 teaspoon cream of tartar

1 teaspoon vanilla extract

1/2 cup sugar

Directions:

1. Preheat the oven to 225°F. Line 2 baking sheets with parchment paper.

2. Combine the egg whites and cream of tartar in a medium bowl and beat at medium speed with an electric mixer until foamy. Beat in the vanilla. Gradually add the sugar and beat at high speed until stiff peaks form.

3. Drop the mixture by rounded tablespoonfuls 1 1/2 inches apart onto the prepared baking sheets. Bake the meringues for 1 hour 15 minutes. Turn off the oven, leaving the meringues inside until completely dry, about 3 hours. The cookies can be stored in an airtight container at room temperature for up to 2 days.

Nutrition Info:

6 g carb, 25 cal, 0 g fat, 0 g sat fat, 0 mg chol, 0 g fib, 1 g pro, 9 mg sod • Carb Choices: 1/2; Exchanges: 1/2 carb

Weeknight Beef And Spinach Lasagna

Servings: 6

Ingredients:

1 teaspoon extra virgin olive oil

8 ounces 95% lean ground beef, crumbled

1 small onion, diced

2 garlic cloves, minced

1 (14 1/2-ounce) can no-salt-added diced tomatoes

1 (8-ounce) can no-salt-added tomato sauce

1/2 teaspoon dried basil

1/2 teaspoon dried oregano

1 cup low-fat cottage cheese

4 ounces shredded part-skim mozzarella (about 1 cup)

1 (10-ounce) package frozen chopped spinach, thawed and squeezed dry

9 no-boil lasagna noodles

2 tablespoons freshly grated Parmesan

Directions:

1. Preheat the oven to 375°F. Brush an 11 x 7-inch glass baking dish with the oil.

2. Combine the beef and onion in a large nonstick skillet. Place over medium heat and cook, stirring often, until the beef is browned, 5 minutes. Add the garlic and cook, stirring constantly, until fragrant, 30 seconds. Add the tomatoes, tomato sauce, basil, and oregano, and bring to a boil. Cook, stirring often, until the sauce is slightly thickened, about 5 minutes.

3. Combine the cottage cheese, mozzarella, and spinach in a medium bowl and stir until well mixed.

4. Spread 3/4 cup of the sauce in the bottom of the prepared baking dish. Place 3 noodles over the sauce, breaking them as needed to fit the dish. Top the noodles with 1 1/2 cups of the cheese mixture and 3/4 cup of the sauce. Repeat the layering, ending with the noodles. Spread the remaining sauce over the top layer of noodles.

5. Cover the baking dish with foil and place the dish on a large rimmed baking sheet. Bake until the noodles are tender, 30 minutes. Uncover, sprinkle the lasagna with the Parmesan, and bake, uncovered, until the Parmesan melts, 5 minutes. Let stand 10 minutes before serving. Cut the lasagna into 6 pieces and serve.

Nutrition Info:

30 g carb, 290 cal, 7 g fat, 4 g sat fat, 36 mg chol, 4 g fib, 22 g pro, 452 mg sod • Carb Choices: 2; Exchanges: 1 1/2 starch, 1 veg, 1 medium-fat protein, 2 lean protein

Cornmeal Muffins with Fresh Cranberries

Servings: 12

Ingredients:

2 teaspoons plus 2 tablespoons canola oil, divided

1 cup fine-grind yellow cornmeal

1 cup unbleached all-purpose flour

1/2 cup sugar

2 teaspoons baking powder

1/2 teaspoon baking soda

1/4 teaspoon salt

1 cup low-fat buttermilk

1 large egg

2 teaspoons grated orange zest

1/2 teaspoon vanilla extract

3/4 cup fresh cranberries or unthawed frozen cranberries

Directions:

1. Preheat the oven to 375°F. Brush a 12-cup muffin tin with 2 teaspoons of the oil or omit the oil and line the tin with paper muffin liners.

2. Combine the cornmeal, flour, sugar, baking powder, baking soda, and salt in a large bowl and whisk to mix well. Combine the buttermilk, remaining 2 tablespoons oil, the egg, orange zest, and vanilla in a medium bowl and whisk until smooth. Add the buttermilk mixture to the cornmeal mixture and stir just until moistened. Gently stir in the cranberries.

3. Spoon the batter evenly into the muffin cups. Bake until a toothpick inserted into the centers of the muffins comes out clean, 25 to 28 minutes.

4. Cool the muffins in the pan on a wire rack for 5 minutes. Remove the muffins from the pan and place on the rack. Serve hot, warm, or at room temperature. The muffins can be stored in an airtight container at room temperature for up to 2 days or frozen for up to 3 months.

Nutrition Info:

28 g carb, 165 cal, 4 g fat, 0 g sat fat,19 mg chol, 1 g fib, 4 g pro, 200 mg sod • Carb Choices: 2; Exchanges: 2 carb, 1 fat

Spinach Salad with Nut-crusted Goat Cheese

Servings: 8

Ingredients:

1/4 cup hazelnuts, toasted and finely chopped

1 (8-ounce) log goat cheese

2 tablespoons seedless strawberry jam

2 tablespoons orange juice

1 tablespoon hazelnut oil or olive oil

1 tablespoon sherry vinegar or white wine vinegar

1/4 teaspoon kosher salt

1/8 teaspoon freshly ground pepper

16 cups torn fresh spinach or baby spinach

2 cups fresh strawberries, hulled and halved

Directions:

1. Place the hazelnuts in a shallow dish and roll the goat cheese in the nuts to coat, pressing to adhere.

2. Whisk together the jam, orange juice, oil, vinegar, salt, and pepper in a large bowl.

3. Add the spinach and strawberries and toss to coat. Divide the spinach among 8 plates. Cut the goat cheese into 8 slices and top each salad with a slice of cheese. Serve at once.

Nutrition Info:

10 g carb, 186 cal, 13 g fat, 6 g sat fat, 22 mg chol, 3 g fib, 9 g pro, 229 mg sod •
Carb Choices: 1⁄2; Exchanges: 1⁄2 carb, 1 high-fat protein, 1 fat

Cilantro-ginger Rub

Servings: About 1/3 Cup

Ingredients:

1/2 cup fresh cilantro leaves

1/4 cup sliced scallions

2 garlic cloves, chopped

1 tablespoon chopped fresh ginger

1 jalapeño, seeded and chopped

1 tablespoon lime juice

2 teaspoons canola oil

1/4 teaspoon Asian sesame oil

1/2 teaspoon kosher salt

1/2 teaspoon chili-garlic paste

Directions:

1. Combine all the ingredients in a food processor and process until finely chopped.

Nutrition Info:

2 g carb, 31 cal, 3 g fat, 0 g sat fat, 0 mg chol, 0 g fib, 0 g pro, 169 mg sod • Carb Choices: 0; Exchanges: 1/2 fat

Pumpkin-cranberry Bread

Servings: 16

Ingredients:

1 teaspoon plus 1/3 cup canola oil, divided

Unbleached all-purpose flour for dusting the pan

1 cup fresh cranberries or unthawed frozen cranberries

2 cups whole wheat flour

3/4 cup sugar

2 teaspoons baking powder

2 teaspoons pumpkin pie spice

1/2 teaspoon baking soda

1/2 teaspoon salt

1 cup canned pumpkin (not pumpkin pie filling)

1/2 cup low-fat buttermilk

2 large eggs

2 teaspoons vanilla extract

Directions:

1. Preheat the oven to 350°F. Brush a 8 1/2 x 4 1/2-inch loaf pan with 1 teaspoon of the oil. Dust the pan lightly with the all-purpose flour, shaking the pan to remove the excess.

2. Place the cranberries in a food processor and pulse 4 or 5 times or until coarsely chopped. Set aside.

3. Combine the whole wheat flour, sugar, baking powder, pumpkin pie spice, baking soda, and salt in a large bowl and whisk to mix well. Combine the remaining 1/3 cup oil, the pumpkin, buttermilk, eggs, and vanilla in a medium bowl and whisk until smooth. Add the pumpkin mixture and the cranberries to the flour mixture and stir just until moistened. (The batter will be very thick.)

4. Spoon the batter into the prepared pan and bake until a wooden toothpick inserted in the center of the loaf comes out clean, 50 to 55 minutes.

5. Cool the bread in the pan on a wire rack for 10 minutes. Remove from the pan and cool completely on a wire rack before slicing. The bread can be stored in an airtight container at room temperature for up to 2 days or frozen for up to 3 months.

Nutrition Info:

24 g carb, 162 cal, 6 g fat, 1 g sat fat, 27 mg chol, 3 g fib, 4 g pro, 180 mg sod •
Carb Choices: 1 1/2; Exchanges: 1 1/2 carb, 1 fat

Roasted Fennel with Pernod

Servings: 4

Ingredients:

2 large bulbs fennel

2 teaspoons plus 1 tablespoon extra virgin olive oil, divided

1/4 teaspoon plus 1/8 teaspoon kosher salt, divided

Pinch of freshly ground pepper

2 teaspoons Pernod or other anise liqueur

1 teaspoon lemon juice

1/8 teaspoon sugar

Directions:

1. Preheat the oven to 425°F.

2. Trim the tough outer stalks from the fennel bulbs. Cut each one in half vertically and discard the cores. Cut each half lengthwise into 1/2-inch slices.

3. Place the fennel in a large roasting pan. Drizzle with 2 teaspoons of the oil and sprinkle with 1/4 teaspoon of the salt and the pepper. Toss to coat. Arrange the fennel in a single layer. Roast, stirring once, until the fennel is tender and lightly browned, 25 to 30 minutes.

4. Meanwhile, whisk together the Pernod, lemon juice, sugar, and remaining 1/8 teaspoon salt in a small bowl. Slowly whisk in the remaining 1 tablespoon oil.

5. Arrange the fennel on a serving plate and drizzle with the Pernod mixture. Serve hot or at room temperature.

Nutrition Info:

10 g carb, 97 cal, 6 g fat, 1 g sat fat, 0 mg chol, 4 g fib, 1 g pro, 166 mg sod • Carb Choices: 1/2; Exchanges: 2 veg, 1 fat

Alphabetical Index

CPSIA information can be obtained
at www.ICGtesting.com
Printed in the USA
BVHW042307060621
608923BV00008B/451